No Mountains Around Here Are Purple

A collection of poems by
George "Hoey" McEwen

Foreword by Dr. Bobbi Lancaster

Edited by Kally Reynolds
and Marybeth Murray

Cover, layout and illustrations
by Jackie Casey

ii

iv

Doggone
And long gone...
"I'll Be Doggone" by Marvin Gaye

This book is dedicated to
The Lord Jesus Christ—
without His love I'd be
Doggone and
Long gone—
and to Catherina Armour,
the love of my life.

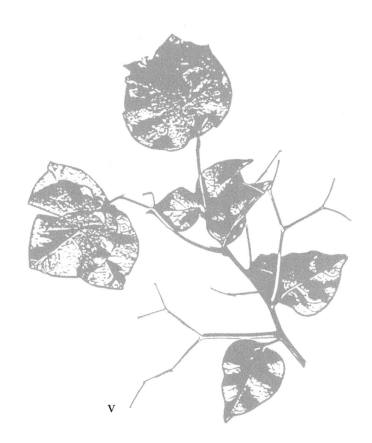

Table of Contents

Foreword...ix

Introduction..xv

Mr. Feral Cat with His Whiskers Licked..........................1

After Some Time...2

Paper Not Needed...4

No Mountains Around Here are Purple.........................6

The Blind Man's Shot..9

Hunger No Fun...11

The Memory of Respect...12

Scraps from the Wind..15

A Bribe in the Confessional......................................16

Darkness in a Vise..19

Takin' a Break..20

The Circus Takes a Detour.......................................23

Anywhere But Here You Can Play..............................24

The Abandoned Cabin and the Waif...........................26

Birthday Hoops..29

East of White Clay..31

A Wish for Sleep in Lamb's Wool (Smiles in Brown Eyes) 32

The Answer to the Weight..................................35

A Break in the Laughter.....................................36

Fresh Milk on a Dog's Whiskers..........................38

Different Times...41

Indian Leaves...42

Daylight Turning Longer....................................45

A Handshake for Your Soul................................46

Many a Chase...49

Happy Laughs for Claudia and Jenny..................51

Christy...53

The Night Stayed Late.......................................54

Fall Talks...58

Acknowledgments...60

The Creative Team..64

Foreword
By Dr. Bobbi Lancaster

Three unopened letters rested on the left side of my desk. They had been addressed to Kally Reynolds, a patient of mine, but they were intended for me. I'm a busy family physician, with not enough time in the day, and opening this correspondence became an obligation of low priority. Kally had told me about her brother, Hoey, who was now the recipient of hospice care. And how she had sent him a book I'd written—my memoir—to help him pass the time, while he waited for an appointment with his Maker.

She repeatedly asked if I'd opened the letters, and I finally experienced a brief pause in my life—my windshield needed replacement. In the quiet of the repair shop waiting room, I tore open the first envelope. The contents spilled onto my lap: old stamps depicting famous golfers—yes, I'd played professional golf at one time; comic book strips that had been methodically cut out from a local newspaper; a card congratulating me on the publishing of my book, and poems that the sender wanted to share with me. I opened these folded poems from this stranger called Hoey, and found myself spellbound from the first stanza.

He wrote about a potpourri of topics: the Seasons; a feral cat with whiskers licked; respect; the mind-numbing nature of blue collar work; anonymity; love lost; Hell; laughter; a circus, and so much more. I read and reread the poems, tore open the second and third envelopes, and rejoiced when I discovered even more poems.

Where did this unheralded writer learn how to juxtapose incongruent words, and turn them into images and themes that somehow make total sense? His phrasing was equally unexpected, and this reader was constantly kept off balance. Hoey's descriptions and unlikely metaphors pack a punch. They are unique, exquisite and sublime... and... I'm searching for the right word here. In the end, these evocative poems touched me deeply. At some point, I realized I was under the spell of an undiscovered rare talent who possessed an almost preternatural ability to communicate.

And then I stepped back, and was finally able to see an over-arching theme to this impressive collection: Hoey, this newfound genius, was a troubled soul, and his poems were autobiographical. He'd lived a laborer's life full of endless and mindless tasks. He was misunderstood; out-of-place; alone; suffering, and romantically dreamed of being taken in and understood—like the Waif and the abandoned dog that he writes about.

Perhaps it will be Mr. Summer or Mr. Fall who will

embrace him in his darkest moments, and shield him from the sharp bite of the approaching Mr. Winter. Or maybe it will be God, whom he has not given up on... yet. I found myself crying for this stranger that had come into my life. I related to him because he is a lot like everyone I know, including me.

Why had he written these poems to begin with? Were they meant to be therapeutic? Was it his way of working through unresolved issues? He certainly was not looking for sympathy. And why had he shared them with me—someone he'd never met, except that he'd read my book? I had so many questions, so I called Kally and got his phone number.

His voice was husky and soft, and there was an out-of-breath cadence to his conversation—after all, he was on oxygen. I introduced myself and we talked for almost an hour. Hoey and I soon learned that we shared a love for sports and especially the game of golf: we had both been caddies too, in our youth. He did not sound like the author of the poems. Rather, he spoke using ordinary words. Hoey demonstrated a ready laugh, and described himself in a humble and self-deprecating manner. The conversation was easy, like we were old friends, and he shared a couple of secrets that I don't believe he's told another human being. He'd obviously bonded with me after reading my life story, and trusted me enough to share his poems and other intimate details. Our relationship was on the fast track, because everything gets expedited when one is on hospice. I found his compliments about my writing style hard to accept because when it comes to his writing, he soars with the angels.

We've shared many long distance conversations since—Hoey lives out of state—and I've given him encouragement and a little medical advice too. Most important, I presented my most convincing argument as to why the world should read his very personal poems. I told him his stories would provide comfort and inspiration for others who struggle. He did not require any arm twisting.

Now we are in a race against Time, and Time is not Hoey's friend. Kally was enlisted, took charge, and Hoey came up with a title: *No Mountains Around Here Are Purple*. What an intriguing name for a book, open to multiple interpretations, and totally in keeping with the man behind the poems. Don't be fooled by his unassuming manner—this Hoey runs deep.

And then he requested I write the foreword for his life's work, and now I'll be part of his legacy too. I am truly honored to introduce Hoey to the universe. You are about to be touched by his observations and his unique compositions. At the time of this writing, the book is being hurried along, and Hoey is still with us. COVID-19 is preventing any possible travel to actually meet my newest friend. Perhaps we'll play a round of golf together in some future meeting place. I suspect the backdrop will be a very *purple mountain*. Hoey... you are amazing.

And I wish you could write at least one last poem, because I sense you have something more to say.

Introduction

As a quiet guy, writing this introduction is difficult. Never in my wildest dreams—and I've had some pretty wild dreams—did I think that my poetry would be in print. Be that as it may, I am a die-hard Chicago Bears fan and get along, especially with dogs and children. I recently took it on the chin with cancer, and most of my activities (including robbing banks and soaping windows on Halloween), I can't do. But anyway, I get along well and have lived longer than the doctors thought. I am a quiet guy, yet I write.

When I am asked why I write poetry, it seems to some people I am dodging the question. Well, I wish I could dodge it more but can't; for when brief and mercurial thoughts come into my mind, I must put them down, so others know they are not alone. I am not sure if I'll write another poem. God works in mysterious ways. I don't know what's going to happen.

Thoughts just come to me about a line and, later, it leads into another one; then I let it go. Being a laborer, my hands don't really know how to let go; but when they do, it feels great. Yet, all those years, I was just happy to have a job.

But then after a job was done, I'd think of other places and times and of what I wished would be. I believe in

Utopia—Eden (and for those familiar with the Chicago area, I don't mean the Eden's Expressway). I don't see why it can't happen down here on Earth. Just what makes it impossible?

My first poem was in either 1976 or 1977. I just did it. Some people liked it and encouraged me. There wasn't a lot of encouragement in my family back then, except from my mom. Still, writing runs in my family. My brother Bob, a retired English professor, has published a number of short stories and poetry books, and both my sisters, Kally and Lynn, write too.

In 1976 I got out of the service and tried to put on a happy façade. I kept myself private. In 1978, my mom died and I haven't cried completely; that sadness still flows around somewhere inside me. Sadness and melancholy poked their noses into my soul, and it comes out in some of my poetry.

By and large, I write a poem for my own satisfaction. I want to contribute. I share it with a friend or two. Friends encourage me to write. I didn't know some poems would be chosen for this collection—but being sick for a while, you learn to get along and save your efforts for more important things. I write them and let them go.

I've struggled with some poems, others have come easy. Sometimes, it is hard to get started or to know when a poem is finished. But when I make my point, I'm done.

Respectfully,

George "Hoey" McEwen

Mr. Feral Cat with His Whiskers Licked

The late May wind comforted
    the here and now.
The waft of innocence was before us
    with the unfurling of playfulness.
Mother Nature had relaxed and let her guard down.
      Yow!

The late May wind put Mr. Time
    on probation.
The beaches and swing sets
    winked to make reparations.
The sound of tears forgot to come around.
      Yow!

The late May wind would bring sandwiches,
    and smiles would appear in a cooler,
      filled with lemon wiles and a plan for after dark.
Forgotten was the feel of locked doors.
Now, the certitude of the beatitudes!
      Yow!

The late May wind brought a harmony,
    the rhythms and beats were in color
      and the colors were sublime.
The dancing and the foxtrot were about to commence.
Mr. Feral Cat slowly started to hum (whiskers were
licked),
        "O stay late, Mr. Late May wind.
        O stay late by the waters awhile."
      Yow!

After Some Time

After some time,
    the cadences of the wind will soften.
Tension will be eased out of a harness of hardness.
Cobwebs will collapse,
    and smiles will arise on a catnip spring day.
A home will be on the horizon.

After some time,
    the radiance of a winter dance will feel like aloe,
    aglow with the texture of once upon a time.
Clandestine conversations concerning a soul
    will be heard under a mosaic moon.
Another chance for crayons, cartoons
    and Christmas carols!
A home with a barn will be on the horizon.

After some time,
    the chill of the scar will subside.
The welcome wagon will deliver hot chocolate, beach balls,
    balm and a map to the entrance of a smile.
A laugh on behalf of the past.
A home with a barn and a dog barking will be on
the horizon.

After some time,
    spoken words will be heard
    and not neglected to irrelevance.

A cupboard of dreams will be opened and shared.
A cagey campfire will appear with a wink
    from the distance.

Around the bend,
    a home with a barn and a dog barking at meadowlarks
    will come into view.

A calico cat will be seen chewing
    on the scenery of serenity.

Time for being lost will be on the mend.

Paper Not Needed

He wasn't a guy who sat around reading about his
press clippings.
For two reasons:

> One – he couldn't read.
> Two – he had no press clippings.

He wasn't a guy who stood around talking about his
press clippings.
For two reasons:

> One – he was often off balance with words.
> Two – he had no press clippings.

He wasn't a guy who lost sleep dreaming about his
press clippings.
For two reasons:

> One – his dreams were of a jocular nature: a
rapture of quiet clowns and canaries reading in a
library; a palm tree with a tiger on the top, drinking a
soda pop, and a young girl writing colors in her diary.
> Two – his dreams had no intuition of any press
clippings.

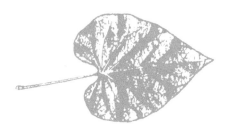

He was a man who met the day before dawn.
The fatigue of yesterday was long gone with a yawn.
Onto the day! Where the sickle meets the hay.
The horse pulls the plow, and everything is now.

The sunrise spoke softly in words easy to learn.
"Harsh, mild, rough and tough, with many an
unforeseen burn. It is your turn to make another
stand. Mister, thanks! I know you understand."

The day progressed, and echoed sounds abounded.
A "Caw-Caw" from the crow. A "Bark-Bark" from the
hound. And a whisper in the clover from the doe. His
words to the horse were spoken in Morse Code:

Dot-Dot-Click-Dot-Click-Dot-Dash-Splith-Splash.

Translated: "If we keep up this steady pace, we'll be
done before sundown and watch God paint another
masterpiece in the sky, knowing the seasons each
have their particular why."

Of course! Oats and apples for you!

No. He didn't know much about paper, nor the
pantomimes of glad hands waiting to use the saber.
But the lemmings waited, a day from going berserk.
They waited, just to see him work.

No Mountains Around Here Are Purple

Chuckles and a cool soapy shower
    were well deserved
    after that dream in the netherworld.

My brother was climbing the tree of no smiles.
He had his rope and his wiles.
He had gloves but no hands.
He had boots and a conscious tooth,
    to remind him nothing is sweet.

He was running through the junkyards of heaven
    shouting: "Trick or Treat."

A skeleton lost the key.
An albino owl said, "We shall see what the sea
    says of the color of your memory:
    maybe midnight is white or
    maybe the weight of migrants
    turning over the bus
    in the sunrise of blight.

But the color is red, white and syruple.
No mountains around here are purple."

The rain died and a cactus smiled
    and said, "Good luck to the Riviera
    via the Chicago ghetto."

A rodeo appeared with brass knuckles,
    wine bottles and tire irons.

Clowns were maimed and butterflies were chained;
    busy beavers got their teeth knocked loose
        by a gang of one-wing ducks with
        gestapo boots.

A rocking chair was used all the time,
    with aged eyes weaving a fabric of hope
    made out of an age-old bout
    of shakes, shallow smiles and the big gallows.

A frosty camel walked by and said,
    "Adios, broken branch boy."

Seals in sunglasses said, "Sayonara."

God said to hombre Roberto, "The nightmare is over.
    Mr. Box Elder and his friends say hello
    to you and yours in a quiet wind."

The Blind Man's Shot

The guy next to me is starving.
Some other guy, his beer and luck, is fading like hell.
Some guy next to me ain't been with a girl
    since cats stayed in at night.

This guy next to me carries a gun,
    kinda like somebody's gonna die.

That guy there who just left gave me his car.

Buddies who travel in snow together
    don't forget the trail.

Guys I work with help my soul
    and re-kindle brotherhood.

Praise the Lord forever!
My laugh is for your kindness, brothers.

Give change to the blind man,
Give biscuits to his best four-legged buddy.

Give the blind man his shot.

Hunger No Fun

It's surprising what a hot
    meal can do!

Yes sir,
    it quiets an angry mind.
    It quiets a dangerous body.

These fasts are okay, but when
    imposed because of
    no money, boys,
    that type of fast is rough.

Tigers don't go hungry for
    very long.

Some people do.
Problems in ego come in second
    and last
    to the despair of no food.

Jokes and smiles need
    not apply
    to people on the growl prowl
    for substance.

Long distance between feeds
    and my idea of fun.

It must be twice as hell for
    the kids.

The Memory of Respect

The wolves were kept at bay
by a bottle of Bay Rum and one tough son of a gun.
But when push comes to shove,
the fangs and fury will not be undone.

The wolves were kept at bay
by a woman with a chinchilla smile.
A zip gun was in her hands, and her hands were dry.

The wolves were kept at bay
by the bombs in Beirut and
the perennial poverty in East Chicago Heights.
The children's screams curled their fur.
The wolves ran far into the night
and were lost between wrong and right.

The wolves were kept at bay
by hollow mirrors and children with skeleton shivers.
The wolves ran, confused.
Who, they thought, could be so amused?

Mr. Number One wolf sprang and spoke,
"I want to meet that one tough son of a gun
who smells nice. I know he hears the hell of
the hatred that always seems to swell.
Before he speaks, he will think twice."

The wolves and the man met without fear.
In the circle of thoughts,
the memory of respect was mourned in tears.

Scraps from the Wind

There is slim chance for sun-up
    when the pall of the call
    quicksands the Fall
    to a
    barbed wire Winter.

No room at the inn
    to the residents of Lower Wacker Drive
    who are still alive
    praying for anything—maybe even a bribe—
    for the last glimpse of
    four walls and a wooly blanket.

The stains of their stunted shadows
    stampede the stiletto sleep
    they have left
    right in the middle of
    a mother's weep.

Good luck to you guys with none.
The old man with ice in his eyes
    is lacing up his boxing gloves—with a horseshoe—
    six feet and under,
    the prize
    for Lower Wacker's frozen cries.

A Bribe in the Confessional

I'll tell you what, Father,
    rather than some hushed words
    and some hocus-pocus motions,

I will give five hundred buckaroos to the poor box
    and throw in one hundred clams
    for Chinese chow at the mission tonight.

If that's alright—Dim lake shrimp with wide-eyed rice—
    delivered from Wang's C Delight.

I will build a gym.
I will even throw in a horse trail
    for the little ones who are frail,
    but as brave as a battleship
    under a hurricane whip.

A pool to swim!
A silo of potato chips
    with plenty of cheddar cheese dip.

I know you are tight with the Big Man upstairs.

I have had many days stained in vain,
    dark is the weather vane.

How about a new Salvation Army with buckets of
    fried chicken and a lot of gravy?

A water park where the waves are always wavy?
For I believe my soul is in jail.

The priest's voice sounded quiet, without glee,
    like a winter's afternoon park about to go dark.

"For your penance, my son,
    shake hands with a rattlesnake.

Go left and then fake a right
    into the path of a moving Mack truck.

Past poisons can be absolved,
    dissolved in forgotten distance from the Deity.

Saying you are sorry paves the way for the salve.

But, in here, you, Bucky, are out of lucky.
Bury your greed with your eyes closed
    and you will find your key."

P.S. Say hi in Needles Eye, New Mexico.
I heard that camels there
    feel the echoes of their souls.

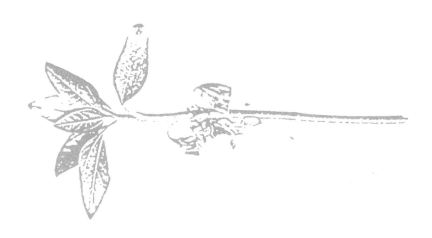

Darkness in a Vise

The slings and arrows and the canceled
   tomorrows remained on duty.

Brightness would be checked at the door.
Hope was punch drunk,
   passed out on the floor.

The nightmarish knaves began to assemble.
Places of Eden were a myth.
A stillborn. A colt alone in the storm.
Encouragement and worth were kicked to the curb.

The line for pats on the back was dense and dark.
Footsteps were mute.
Indifference was sold with an easy price tag of
   "No thanks."
The bank was closed. The crow cawed.

Darkness in a vise and the vise is
   Cold.

Takin' a Break

Cold cities sometimes turn colder
    around this time.

Mangers turn damp.
Guys with newspapers wet
    around them
    can read all the pages
    at once.

Employment section
    got no jobs for guys who
    ain't sticking around.

Winter sure feels better
    in a warm home.

Coziness, grub cookin', and me
    and you, just sittin' around,
    sippin' wine and beer,
    hypnotizing the shepherd to
    dog-dreamland
    with quiet scratches.

Railroad men say
    "The sun always shines on the railroad."

By that they mean that you'd
    better pretend,
    because you're going
    to have to work anyway.

Give the ball to the Windy Hawk.
Hoey and his shepherd
    takin' a break
    Winter '81.

The Circus Takes a Detour

Locked doors in a locked house,
    the ghoul in the window peers out.

A sunless sun slings a loaded gun of venom
    with enough bullets of bitterness
    to make the alleys appear clean.

How did this malignant malice
    make its way into the palace
    of what had been a happy home
    where laughter once was real?

Was it no water, no food
    or was it that
    she was made to feel no good?

A one-armed doll.

The heart's answer trespasses logic,
    but not the toxic chills of a child cowering
    over long speechless days,
    dreams in disarray, smiles gone quickly away.

The circus takes a detour
    a million miles from her.

Anywhere But Here You Can Play

Something broke when the yells
    turned into anger,
    the play became work
    and the work was hell.

Something broke when the yells
    turned into slaps.

The nightmares were at night,
    and the night was all day.

Something happened when the yells
    turned into beatings.

The boogey man showed up in the mornings
    and the morning begat unheard weepings:
    Fourth-grade fist fights
    Ninth-grade auto theft
    Eleventh-grade nickel-and-dime diners.

Something broke when the yells
    locked a lonely door,
    and time graduated to its logical roar.

The switchblade took a handgun,
    and the handgun dismissed an innocent man
    from the fun of a blue sky.

Wrong place, wrong time, sorry, guy.

Something broke when the yells
   turned the gas chamber into a
   pitch-black goodbye.

The mother, brother
   and the one on the Cross cried.

The Abandoned Cabin and the Waif*

The Waif's sated smiles started towards a sleepy nod, when there began a thumping and bumping onto the cabin's door. A coldness seeped onto the cabin's floor. A chillness leapt into the window sills like a wounded ghost. Whatever that was moving or stirring in sweat would be felt by the Waif's touch. Here was another chance of giving.

The Abandoned Cabin felt a reunion of hope of times past; the loom in the sewing room started to blink. The kitchen began to make ready: knives, plates and water bowls came on alert. The atmosphere within the walls started to percolate; the phonograph winked. The Waif heard his pulse quicken like a kite.

Opening the entrance to the Abandoned Cabin (getting less by each miracle!), there was a dog! By God! Mercy! A halo showed in the dark. His heart could be seen through his brown eyes, unforgettable, in the sadness of unwanted goodbyes. His tired and thatched soul had carried him many a mile. There were frozen tears embedded in his fur.

The cabin sighed and started to shore up his strength. His fire and warmth began to expand. He began to assemble healing feelings to the Waif's finger tips.

"Help this warrior in, Raif. Our new friend looks more beat up then you did a ways back. Let us help him to forget some scents that left more than a few rough dents. Away from the long fast slaps that left little chance to escape the whip.

"You know where the spare pillows, blankets and lullabies are. He will need some warm soapy washing —Gently ahem—around dawn.

"His slumber will rest in here now; his plundered soul now has a home. Time will be given to this Shepherd who only wants someone to give a smile to. Time to be listened to and not asking why. Time for a hayride under an azure blue sky."

*an excerpt from a longer work

Birthday Hoops

All by myself with no one to play with,
    no one to talk with;
    bad trouble and me met
    when I was a kid.

Friends mean the most to me.

Say, Bob, let's me and you climb
    up that tree and frisk those robins.
    (I'm just kiddin'.)

Say, Bob, you're my brother
    who has given me
    the quietness of the Bobkat butterfly,
    cozy ears and plenty of honey.

I'll climb anywhere for you.

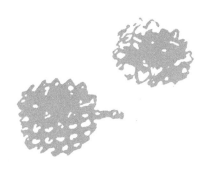

East of White Clay

In the nick of time I got
    saved by the invisible dog.

When we were
    small guys, we got sent
    to the corner of the circle,
    but neither of us could find it.

So we kinda' thithered and worked,
    him as a watch dog,
    me a laborer.

What counts is our addition,
    its blankets are simple:
    one plus one.

Shep's easy paws blaze many a path
    to chocolate-chip heaven,
    and I'm home for him too.

Some girl we met,
    shadows ago,
    talked horses and had
    other ideas and left (darn it)
    right to the crossroads
    of nowhere.

East of White Clay.

A Wish for Sleep in Lamb's Wool
(Smiles in Brown Eyes)

A family and me (Uncle Hoey)
    once laughed as horsey-back rides never stopped.

Uncle Hoey's horsey-back bounces
    flavored the trail of tomorrow's sun.

A snicker and a wink for fun
    were all that mattered.

Sometimes his nieces needed a ride
    to a sky-high slumbered sleep,
    Mother Goose books and eyes that took
    no memory of a sorrowed weep.

Bucking and swaying the little ones
    until the moon bays,
    away from a yesterday
    that no one can understand.

"Hee, Hee, Hee."
Uncle Hoey's horsey-back glee
    sure isn't tired.

Many an empty manger
    was filled by you.

No thoughts of danger, just delight.

Days go by.
Dreams still say hi
    to the ones with smiles in brown eyes.

Pieces of love that are in my heart,
    a new day, always with a robin's hop-start
    to a horsey-back past.

The Answer to the Weight

"Why was Mom's casket so heavy,
    Uncle Hoey? I saw you straining
    to gain steps to the hearse,
    while I took the last few tissues from my purse."

"Beautiful princess, whose future is bold,
    your mother's heart was heavy with gold,
    the gold only mined in:

    storybooks and sea-shell smiles;
    parades of ponies and late night talks;
    carnivals of cotton-candy and early morning walks;
    and the Saturday night curry chicken that tasted
    like calypso music played on a prairie winter night.

"She left these treasures for you and
    your darling sisters, and for all the animals
    (and us) with or without whiskers.
She left wooly blankets for a chilly night and
    and a wake-up kiss to make the daylight bright.
She left gold to remind you of your true worth
    up in heaven and here on earth.

"Why was your mom's casket so heavy, my princess?
...It was heavy with her love."

A Break in the Laughter

His laugher came down through his eyes
   like a snowy Christmas Eve.

The moment now was happiness.
Mirth was up his sleeve.
He was a nice guy helping a quiet kid
   on a summer's fire-fly night.

Lord, have mercy.
   I didn't know what
   was so funny
   as toughness in hardship.

But he did.
The old stories were still new to him.

Times' past shook his Serengeti soul.
   Remembrances of close calls
   and some
   six feet under.

Dandelions looking up.
A break in the laughter.

Then he continued:
   Frolics under shady trees. Ha! Ha! Ha!
   Winter nights, and you and me. Ho! Ho! Ho!
   A campsite with a fire bright. Hee! Hee! Hee!

Taking a hiccup hike to a slow freight
    into a town that had some work.

Ladies long, with long memories.
Aces high with quick hands.
A late morning's sleep.

    Haw! Haw! Haw!

Dogs bark mightily.
Cats nap kingly.
Horses trot like solitary soldiers
    in servitude to the stench
        they see with long hidden brown eyes.

A break in the laughter.

Hoops shot in Southern Illinois.
Football caught in Louisville.
Baseballs hit in Mobile.
A woman's love from Holland.
A beagle's welcome from a rough go.

These joys carried
    him happily
    past some sorry
    slum sorrows that held
    a break in the laughter.

Fresh Milk on a Dog's Whiskers
———————————————

Another tough one to take.
I thought I had a chance.
Not today, Hoey.
She's got another guy.

Maybe when Hell freezes over,
    or I stop drinking,
    or leave my shirt on
    in the Summer and Winter.

A roofer once told me
    it doesn't matter if you fall
    50 feet or 500, you're
    still going to kill yourself.

I cried out at midnight
    hoping your eyes and warmth
    would be there.
Maybe I should learn to cry with tears.

Old expressions comfort
    me like a hot cup of coffee.
But new phrases mock me,
    such as "Mademoiselle."

Once in the land of No-Trails,
    I found it easy to speak.

My feet were sure and tough.
I had a hat for my ears.

Sister Wolf came and offered
    me some food.

I thought I had it made.
I felt I had it made.

Fresh milk on a dog's whiskers
    had nothing on me.

Different Times

Coarse sweat on a coarse man.
Quiet meadow creeks chocked full
   of meadow kats
    that give no contentment in thought.

Kit Carson is lost
   in the backfield.

I turned to myself for directions,
   but he took off to
   real graves
   and imaginary ideas.

Indian Leaves

So this guy says to me
    "Come on, Hoey.

Speak some of those
    blues that's got you down.

Hoey, open up some.
You were the guy who planted
    that garden
    for the old folks."

Go ahead, Hoey, and walk in your mind.
Go ahead and face some of those
    tears and fears:
    the Dead Maw
    the Dead Dawg
        (my confidante and pal).

My thoughts glazed over
    a plane of my mind that
    I don't want to go.

Go ahead and smoke those
    smokes that go down like candy.

Go ahead and drink those
    beers and cheap wine.

Go ahead and sip that
    Syrup (Knott's Maple) and smoke those
    reefer joints. Play kids' games and
    cancel today and tomorrow.

Go ahead and put your
    imagination in
    your left hand and
    fake out love.

Go ahead and heal the
    Rabid dog.

Go ahead in the Sandhills and
    say, "Yes sir, Boss, I'm on my
    way."

Go ahead and hear
    someone say,
    "I gotta go."

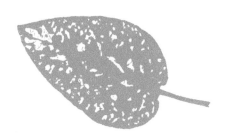

I love a girl with nine
    lives.
The walk in my mind
    leaps to a girl with
    snow shadow eyes.

The worn canvas of my shoes
    tells me
    I've got to get up and go.
All praise to God!

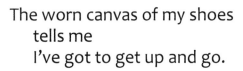

Daylight Turning Longer

When the Spring blossoms, there's a feel in the air:
    Icy cold root beers,
        Hopscotch and moths finding their way home to
        the street corner light.

Trees ready to climb to your sunset, Sweetheart,
    maybe to find an open window and a
    friendly welcome, a just reward.

Winter's debt was paid long ago.

This year, this harbor of Spring secrets
    showed up broken,
    like a bum in the street
    with hands in a pocket of torn cloth
    and dreams that are not sweet.

These little Guys and Gals are
    no street litter.

They wish to feel legs that climb,
    feet that jump,
    and hands to grasp
    the friendly welcome of a well-worn tree.

A Handshake for Your Soul

The distance between destinations defies
    the teardrop of lost cries.
A handkerchief in a closed hand to
    remember what you're trying to forget.
A long step in a small body.

A handshake for your soul.

Time is longer than a coal miner's Mondays,
    whose eyes are awake in sulphur and tombstone,
    hoping to see the sun and a way back home.
(You would probably skip your way to the pick
    and tell the straw boss: "We better turn to:
    daylight is waiting, and she's pretty quick, too,
    with lots of tricks up her sleeves.")

A handshake for your soul.

No hundred-yard dashes will be faster
    —except the fire on cold chains—
    than your snuggled smile
    at an apple-blossom pie
    (the one baked by Elaine),
    that warms the weariness of a
    winter sky.

Your smile is like a July keepsake,
in a summer of space, walking
home at a pleasant pace.

A handshake for your soul.

Fingers born ready to shoot a basketball.
Let us help these kids be out and about.
Laughing like lumberjack larks in a quiet park,
giving us handshakes from their souls
in a grassy green glen.

Many a Chase

Mr. Owl sang the scripture;
    the little ones were in their nest.

The water in the brook was pure;
    honey and milk were the best.

Mr. Afternoon turned still and shy,
    Papa Owl and Mama Owl had thoughts quiet.

Mouskies in the shade were about to die,
    Rabbits in the clover knew the reason why.

Mr. Evening reaped the colors of solitude.
Papa and Mama Owl ended their nap in a state of bliss.

Talons and eyes were sharpened for the right attitude.
"I must rest a bit longer; then I'll go and won't miss."

Mr. Night pounced on what was left of the shadows;
    he knew the spark of the dark would not be seen.

Mr. Owl was in the meadows,
    the circuits of his symmetry were keen.

The nourishment of life was brought home before dawn.
The little ones grateful, left not a trace.

Papa Owl stifled a yawn;
    the years would be splendid with many a chase.

Happy Laughs for Claudia and Jenny

Comfort rests naturally in
    the arms of the young girl,
    her laughter reaches
    straight to her mother's soul;
    they nestle closer.

The child's laughter reawakens
    something in her mother's heart;
    reliving happy moments,
    they laugh together,
    laughs that are true
    and the touch that tells them so.

Always.

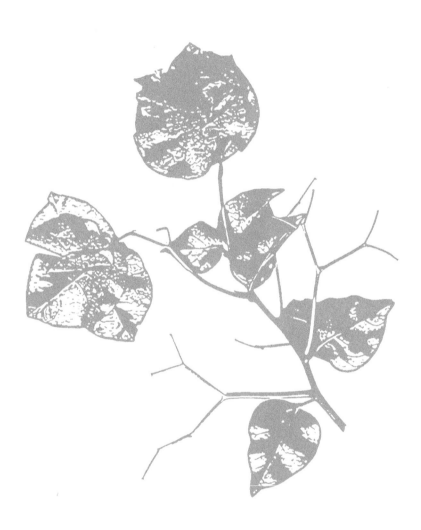

Christy

The youngest son comes in late,
    he was fishing for bait.

A wife and mother,
    she understands. She
    taught ditchdiggers the
    front end of a shovel.

Her name is Christy
    and her kindness shines like a
    bedtime story for the kids.

Christy's love breaks through his boundaries.

Christy, your soul makes
    your kids smile
    and me.

The Night Stayed Late

A roughshod guy walked into a friendly place.
It was as strange as the open range
    would be in a ghetto war zone,
    of rats, ripped windows and
    not knowing how to spell ozone
    or any other library-like words
    that chained his nightmare to the day.

Here was no money without marked aces.

So this friendly place
    saw a defaced
    human being looking for a spark
    that might lead (maybe) to an easy laugh:

    "What is the longest pencil in the world?"
    —Pennsylvania—

    "Who invented the hedgehog hop?"
    —A hedgehog—

    "Why did the chicken cross the road?"
    —Because his boat was in dry dock—

Chuckles and ice-cold lemonade
    tried to open a space and arms
    for this guy who lived his life
    in the siren of an all-day alarm.

"Within these walls, fella, we try to charm
   the cold
   out of a cold night."

    "What does it say on the wings of geese?
      —Honk if you like my flying—

"And, buddy, you look like a hundred blankets
   won't warm
   the slipshot of your fright."

The roughshod guy walked wobbily to a chair
   and wiped his eyes clear
   with the last fold of his shirt
   that held no dirt of dreams
   ending in screams.
No back doors.

A couple of couples and other folks
   came crisply and earnestly up to him.
"We're telling corny jokes.
It makes the wake water easier to swim.
Bartender, a cold lemonade for my friend."

    "What did the octopus say to the platypus?"
      —My, but you do have a sweet puss—

    "What did the father snail say with his son
      to the tortoise at the outhouse?"
    —Would you mind hurrying? 'E's got to go—

The lemonade tasted like a story
    and quenched his worries. A long wish,
    he tried to make a joke
    but only felt joy in his ears.

He actually remembered a joke about
    Yogi the Bear.

But in his eyes were tears.

The night stayed late.
The morning was happy to wait.

Fall Talks

A taffy-apple autumn wide awake
   with a cool blue sky forgetting the rake,
   Mr. Summer smiles serenely and slow.
Now, Mr. Fall will claim his stake.

Evenings darken a little sooner than hoped.
The night is not yet ready to be brief,
   nor yet grant an audience for grief.

Freshness was ready for two for the trail.
Sunrises, sunset,
   the wiles of smiles allured in scents.

Laughter spilling through the leaves
   and chuckles by a campfire breeze,
   Mr. Fall would be a welcome guest.

Yes, sir, my oh my!
Kites and geese on the fly.
Nuts burying chipmunks
   (I mean the other way around).

Still, the unspoken farewells in a tough time swell.
Bad brakes and broken hearts will face Mr. Hell:
   a Saturday-night-special, a blood-stained wing.

Yet, even the garrote of sound
    cannot break the bond
    between us and the angels who sing.

Thanks, Lord, for all of our chances,
    all of the colors in the wild-hyacinth harbor,
    a long walk along heavenly mansions.

Acknowledgments

In deeply felt gratitude to the people below—and the countless other individuals I have not named but are etched in my heart as well—thanks for being in my life. Some of you worked to make this collection of poetry a reality. Others did not even know that it was being published. But I am in debt to all of you—for your kindness, wisdom, and compassion—and most of all for your friendships. You have helped make my life worthwhile.

My sister, Kally, our super orchestra leader, and Jim Reynolds, the silent backbone of this whole operation

My sister, Lynn, who's always had a good word for me

My brother, Bob, who knows the paths of the stars

All the Hospice people, especially Mary Johnson, Tracy Lenard, Cherice Moore and Dino Pelaez

Nick, who took me in

Jay, who kept me alive

Big Mike, Patty, and Ruth Polzin for their lifelong friendship

Maurice, for keeping an eye on me during the week

Marybeth, whose joyous smile is infectious and her help, invaluable

Jackie Casey, who made this book look beautiful

John Terpstra, poet and writer extraordinaire, who read and reviewed this book in record time

Mickey Nelson, who visited and comforted me when I was at my lowest

Amundsum Family and their three angel helpers: Murphy, Madison and Wyatt

Rev. Darlene Cothron, the Reverend with the beautiful voice

All my nieces and nephews

Sam and Jan Cali

Tom Nemith

Doug and DD

John Fountain, writer at the Chicago *Sun-Times*

All my co-workers at Skyline Disposal, especially Chris White

Paco

"Arthur" Pete Carney and Sue

Joel Hirsch

Brimstin and Gillespie families, especially Dash

Irene Lee

Darla Draus

Rebecca and Phil

John ("Big Dog") Kalin

Veronica

Doris Campbell

Tom and Elizabeth

Jake and Janet

Ted Recknagle

Christy

*And to all the stray dogs and stray people—we shared many a laugh

And, finally, a very special thanks to Dr. Bobbi Lancaster for believing in these poems—and me. Without her, this book never would have come into being.

George "Hoey" McEwen

The Creative Team

Kally Reynolds

It's been a dream come true for me to edit and put together a collection of my brother Hoey's poetry. The more I read over his poems, the more I love them. And, best of all, I'm getting to know Hoey better through the powerful poetry he has written. It is a humbling and enthralling experience!

(coachkally@gmail.com)

Bobbi Lancaster, M.D.

Without Dr. Bobbi's vision, Hoey's work would still be languishing in a bulky red notebook in his closet. After reading some of Hoey's poetry, Dr. Bobbi came up with the idea of putting this collection together, and she graciously wrote the foreword for it. Bobbi Lancaster, M.D. is a family physician, author, speaker, Boyce Arboretum Board member and tour guide, retired professional golfer, transgender rights advocate and one of the coolest women on the planet! (plusoneatsixty@hotmail.com)

Jackie Casey

When you take a look at this book, you will see Jackie's creative touches all over it. Jackie is one of those rare creative designers who can take a writing project from start to finish with such ease and grace that she makes it look easy. An artist of many hats—illustrator, comic artist and designer, to name a few—she created the cover, the interior art and the whole "feel" of Hoey's work. She also formatted the book and supplied some of the photographs. (jecruby@gmail.com)

Marybeth Murray

A lover of words and pictures, Marybeth was the person that Hoey called in to make sure his thoughts were honored and accurately communicated. While Marybeth lives near Hoey, the other three of us on Hoey's creative team live more than 1,800 miles away. He couldn't have chosen any-one better! "Hoey used to keep me company with his own created jokes when we worked on service projects together. Then came his poems, and they told me who he was."